A New True Book

EARTHQUAKES

By Helen J. Challand, Ph. D.

*This "true book" was prepared
under the direction of
Illa Podendorf,
formerly with the Laboratory School,
University of Chicago*

CHILDRENS PRESS, CHICAGO

An earthquake caused the land in
the foreground of this picture to sink
ten feet.

PHOTO CREDITS

Office of Earthquake Studies: United States
Geological Survey (USGS)—2, 12, 16, 17,
22 (2 photos), 40, 44, 45

K. Sergerstrom, (USGS)—30 (2 photos)

J. C. Ratte, (USGS)—31 (2 photos)

R. Hoblitt, (USGS)—32

Tony Freeman—4 (top)

Bill Thomas—4 (bottom)

Allan Roberts—11

Len Meents—6, 9, 28, 34

National Oceanic & Atmospheric
Administration (NOAA)—15

Wide World—Cover, 18, 19, 21, 25, 26, 36,
38, 42

COVER—Ruined building after 1964
                    earthquake, Alaska

Library of Congress Cataloging in Publication Data

Challand, Helen J.
    Earthquakes.

    (A New true book)
    Includes index.
    Summary: Briefly describes the earth's interior,
the forces and stresses that sometimes cause the
ground to shake, and the effects of such movement.
    1. Earthquakes—Juvenile literature. [1. Earth-
quakes] I. Title.
QE521.3.C45   1982   551.2'2   82-9699
ISBN 0-516-01636-9   AACR2

TABLE OF CONTENTS

WHAT DOES THE EARTH LOOK LIKE?

The earth is a ball of rocks. It is almost round. Water and land are on top of these rocks.

The large areas of water are called lakes and oceans. The smaller ones are ponds, marshes, and swamps. Long flowing waters are called streams and rivers.

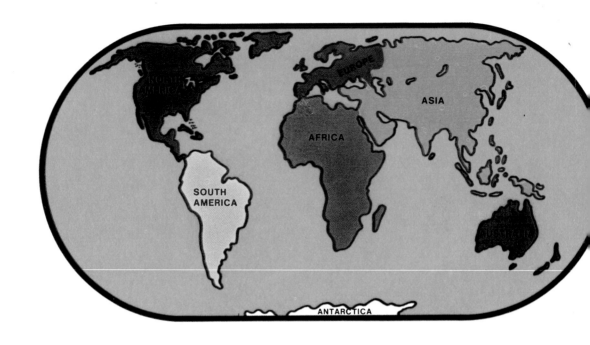

The large land areas are the continents. Today there are seven continents. They are North America, South America, Europe, Asia, Africa, Australia, and Antarctica.

WHAT DID THE EARTH LOOK LIKE LONG AGO?

Two hundred million years ago there was only one large mass of land. The rest of the earth was covered with water.

Slowly this one landmass broke up into smaller pieces. These hunks of land moved only a few inches or feet each year.

WHAT DOES THE EARTH LOOK LIKE ON THE INSIDE?

The inside of the earth has three parts.

The center is called the core. It is about 3,200 miles thick. The core is made of iron and nickel. It is solid and very hot.

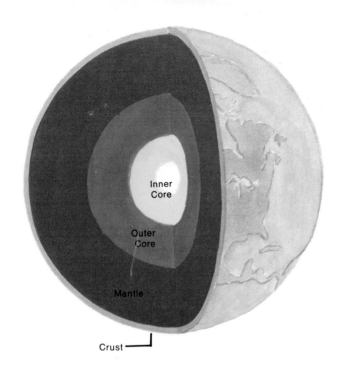

Inner
Core

Outer
Core

Mantle

Crust

The outer part of the core is almost a liquid. Around the core is another layer called the mantle. It is about 1,800 miles thick.

Most of the mantle is made of solid rock. Iron, magnesium, and silicon are found in this rock. A thin layer on the outside of the mantle is very hot. Here the rocks form a thick liquid.

The crust is the outer layer of the earth. It is 0 to 30 miles thick.

In the land areas the crust is usually granite.

Granite mountains

Under the ocean the rocks are made of basalt. Plants, animals, and people live on and in the earth's crust.

After the earthquake in Alaska, 1964

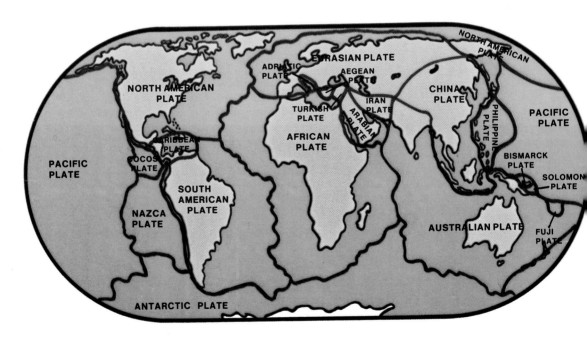

The plates fit together like the pieces of a jigsaw puzzle.

WHAT CAUSES EARTHQUAKES?

Scientists believe that the earth's crust is made of 8 to 12 huge pieces called plates. These plates are made of rock.

These plates are always moving.

The earth is very restless. As the plates move, rocks slide, crack, sink, and groan. Sometimes a huge rock gets caught against another one. The pressure builds up.

Rocks can be stretched and pushed out of shape.

They may not move for years. Pressure builds. A great deal of energy is stored. Finally, the rocks can stand no more pressure. They shake and crumble and cause an earthquake.

An earthquake causes
the air to move. It sounds
like thunder.
Land rises and falls.

Mountains can be split
in half. Hills and bluffs
tumble down. Huge ice
blocks slide down the
sides of mountains.

The cement on the
highways rises up into
large hills. Railroad tracks
twist and buckle.

Cars fall into big holes
in the ground.

Workers cleaning up earthquake damage in California

Buildings tremble and break.

Water and sewer pipes crack open. Power lines and telephone lines fall down.

Often there are fires after a big earthquake.

HOW LONG DOES AN EARTHQUAKE LAST?

An earthquake usually lasts only a few seconds. Some big ones have lasted five minutes. The little tremors or twitches can be felt for days.

Earthquake damage in the village of Santorini (san • tor • EE • nee)

HOW MANY AND HOW BAD ARE THEY?

There are several thousand earthquakes each year. Only about 100 of them are bad.

China has had the worst earthquake so far. In 1556 it shook the earth so hard that 830,000 people were killed.

Earthquake damage in Skoplje (SKOP • la), Yugoslavia (yoo • go • SLAH • via)

A bad earthquake can release as much energy as 2,000 atomic bombs exploding.

HOW STRONG IS AN EARTHQUAKE?

Scientists use an instrument to record the strength of a quake. It is called a seismograph. It

Above: Cross-sectioned seismometer, an instrument used to measure conditions in the earth.
Right: Seismic recorder used to measure aftershocks.

can pick up shock waves as far as 600 miles away.

The waves are measured on a Richter scale. This scale goes from 1 to 9.

A reading of 2 is 30 times stronger than a reading of 1.

If an earthquake measures below 4 on the scale, it usually does not do much damage. When it goes over 7 it causes destruction.

WHAT IS A FAULT?

A fault is a crack in the crust of the earth. It is a scar left by old earthquakes.

A famous fault in California is called the San Andreas Fault. It looks like a valley. It is 600 miles long and is millions of years old.

1906 San
Francisco
earthquake

A big quake happened along this fault on April 18, 1906. The ground moved over ten feet in some places. It caused the famous San Francisco fire.

California has over 100 earthquakes each year. Most of them are small.

The last big one was near San Fernando in 1971. It killed over sixty people.

It did millions of dollars worth of damage to homes and stores. It added four feet to the height of the San Gabriel Mountains.

SAN ANDREAS FAULT

The floating plates that cover the earth are slowly moving. The San Andreas Fault is the line between two plates.

Los Angeles is on a different plate than San Francisco. Los Angeles is on a plate moving north.

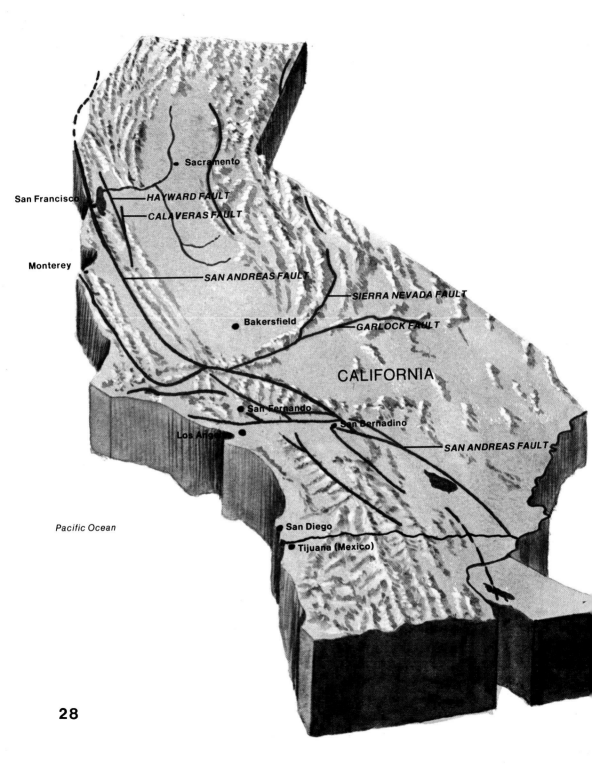

San Francisco

Monterey

Sacramento

HAYWARD FAULT

CALAVERAS FAULT

SAN ANDREAS FAULT

SIERRA NEVADA FAULT

Bakersfield

GARLOCK FAULT

CALIFORNIA

San Fernando

San Bernadino

Los Angeles

SAN ANDREAS FAULT

Pacific Ocean

San Diego

Tijuana (Mexico)

28

San Francisco is on a plate with the rest of the United States. This floating rocky plate is slowly moving south.

Millions of years ago the part of California west of the fault was much farther south. It was once where Mexico is today.

Millions of years from now Los Angeles and San Francisco will be next to each other.

Parícutin (pah • REE • ka • teen) Volcano
erupted in 1943.

EARTHQUAKES
AND VOLCANOES

Earthquakes do not
always make volcanoes.
But volcanoes can make
the earth quake.

A volcano is active when a spot in the earth opens up. Steam, hot gases, and liquid rock spill out. This liquid rock is called lava. It is called magma when it is still inside the ground.

Hawaii is a chain of islands formed by lava.

Lava flow from a 1973 eruption of Mauna Ulu (MAW • nah OO • loo) Crater on the slopes of Kileuea (kee • LOH • ay • ah) Volcano

In 1943 an earthquake in Mexico caused a volcano to form. It started in the middle of a farmer's field. It grew 1,200 feet high in ten years.

Several new islands in Iceland were formed by volcanoes.

Mount St. Helens erupted in 1980

THE RING OF FIRE

Earthquakes are common around the edge of the Pacific Ocean. This rim is called the ring of fire. Many volcanoes are found here. They are caused by earthquakes.

North and South America have earthquakes. They happen in Italy, Greece, India, Iran, and Algeria, too.

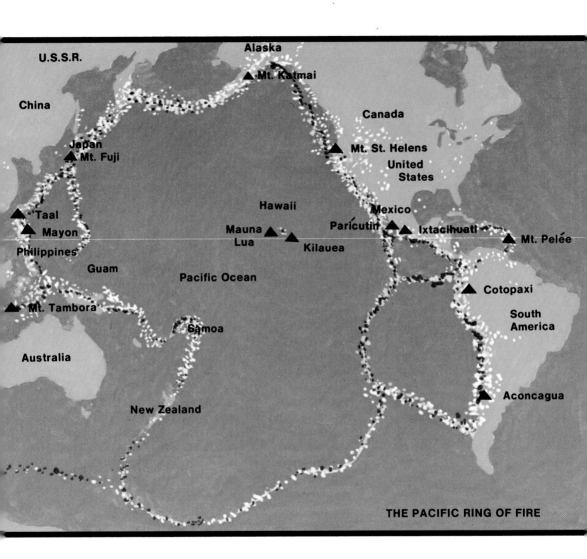

The Pacific Ring of Fire

- U.S.S.R.
- Alaska
- ▲ Mt. Katmai
- China
- Canada
- Japan
- ▲ Mt. Fuji
- ▲ Mt. St. Helens
- United States
- Hawaii
- Mexico
- ▲ Taal
- Parícutin
- ▲ Ixtacihuatl
- ▲ Mayon
- Mauna ▲ ▲ Lua
- ▲ Mt. Pelée
- Philippines
- Kilauea
- Guam
- Pacific Ocean
- Cotopaxi
- ▲ Mt. Tambora
- South America
- Samoa
- Australia
- New Zealand
- ▲ Aconcagua

THE PACIFIC RING OF FIRE

34

On the other side of the Pacific Ocean the ring of fire continues. There are earthquakes in the Philippines, Japan, China, and the Aleutian Islands.

One earthquake in Alaska broke a record. It happened on March 27, 1964. It measured almost 9 on the Richter scale. The ground rose fifty feet. This is higher than most school buildings.

EARTHQUAKES
UNDER THE WATER

Earthquakes can happen under the sea. They can raise or lower the ocean floor.

An earthquake in Chile caused a tidal wave that caused this damage in Hilo, Hawaii 6,800 miles away.

Earthquakes can cause huge landslides under the water. This makes waves. The waves circle out in all directions. They stop when they hit something such as the shore of a continent. These waves have a special name. They are called tsunamis.

After an earthquake these waves may travel for hundreds of miles. They can move at 600 miles an hour. By the time the waves reach a shore they may be 100 feet high. A huge wall of water pours onto the land.

An earthquake in the Gulf of Alaska caused big waves to hit Hawaii. Once a whole city was drowned.

Tidal wave damage on Hawaii

CAN PEOPLE
SHAKE THE EARTH ?

Yes, people have caused earthquakes. This happens when water or wastes are pumped into deep wells. This puts a lot of pressure on and in the rock layers. If it is too great, the rocks will move suddenly. This causes an earthquake.

CAN SOMETHING BE DONE ABOUT EARTHQUAKES?

Scientists believe that someday a safe way can be found to stop the earth from shaking.

Laser ranging instrument used to measure earth changes along a fault line. Over 10,000 earthquakes have been recorded by scientists.

Some kind of liquid could be pumped into faults. This would be like oiling the rocks. The floating plates of rocks would then slide by each other. This would keep them from getting stuck and breaking loose.

Scientist are developing instruments that can measure the slightest tremble. They can even record the creeping along of rocks.

In earthquake areas buildings must be able to withstand shaking. They should be made of steel frames. Concrete walls need metal rods running through them.

During an earthquake wooden houses can bend and sway more than brick ones.

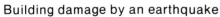
Building damage by an earthquake

MYTHS ABOUT EARTHQUAKES

Today we know what causes earthquakes. But once upon a time people had many wild ideas about what caused them.

Some thought the earth was riding on the back of a giant turtle. When the turtle moved, parts of the earth would crack.

Others thought we were riding a huge frog.

The strangest idea was that the earth was on the head of a bull. People thought there were four bulls. An earthquake was caused when one bull tossed the earth to another bull.

An earthquake caused part of this bridge to collapse.

This damage to Anchorage, Alaska was caused by a 1964 earthquake.

We know now these stories were all myths. Scientist today know why the earth snaps, crackles, and pops.

WORDS YOU SHOULD KNOW

area(AIR • ee • ah) — a section or region.

basalt(bah • SAWLT) — a type of rock formed from lava.

buckle(BUK • ihl) — to bend or twist.

continent(KAHN • tin • ent) — one of the seven main landmasses of the earth.

core(KOR) — the center of the earth.

crust(KRUSST) — the outer layer of the earth surrounding the mantle.

damage(DAM • ij) — to do harm; to destroy.

destruction(deh • STRUK • shun) — damage or serious harm.

earthquakes(irth • KWAKES) — a shaking of the ground caused by sudden movements of rocks underneath the earth's surface.

energy(EN • er • gee) — power to do work.

fault(FAWLT) — a crack in the crust of the earth.

granite(GRAN • it) — a kind of rock that is formed from lava.

huge(HYOOJ) — very big.

hunk — piece.

landslide(LAND • slyde) — the sliding down of a part of the land.

lava(LAH • vah) — hot, melted rock that flows from a volcano.

magma(MAG • mah) — melted rock under the earth's surface.

magnesium(mag • NEE • zee • um) — a metal that is light and fairly hard.

mantle(MAN • till) — the layer of the earth around the core and below the crust.

mass — a large amount or piece.

myth(MITH) — a story that is not true.

plate(PLAYT) — part of the crust of the earth.

predict(prih • DIKT) — to tell what will happen before it happens.

pressure(PRESH • ur) — to put force on something; to push.

San Andreas (SAN an • DRAY • us) **Fault**—the name of a fault in California.

seismic (SIZE • mik)—of or relating to earthquakes.

seismograph (SIZE • me • graf)—an instrument that measures the force of an earthquake.

seisometer (size • OM • iter)—instrument used to measure earth movement.

sewer (SOO • er)—a pipe that carries waste water.

silicon (SILL • ih • cone)—an element found in many of the rocks and minerals of thesarth.

tremble (TREM • bil)—to shake.

tremor (TREM • er)—a shaking or vibrating.

tsunami (soo • NAH • mee)—a very large ocean wave caused by underwater earthquakes.

volcano (vahl • KAY • noh)—an opening in the earth's crust through which lava, dust, ash, and hot gases are thrown.

INDEX

About the Author

Helen Challand earned her M.A. and Ph.D. from Northwestern University. She currently is Chair of the Science Department at National College of Education and Coordinator of Undergraduate Studies for the college's West Suburban Campus.

An experienced classroom teacher and science consultant, Dr. Challand has worked on science projects for Scott Foresman and Company, Rand McNally Publishers, Harper-Row Publishers, Encyclopedia Britannica Films, Coronet Films, and Journal Films. She is associate editor for the Young People's Science Encyclopedia *published by Childrens Press.*